Published by Sterling Publishing Co., Inc.
387 Park Avenue South, New York, NY 10016

© 2006 Nina Chertoff and Susan Kahn

Distributed in Canada by Sterling Publishing
c/o Canadian Manda Group, 165 Dufferin Street,
Toronto, Ontario, Canada M6K 3H6

Distributed in the United Kingdom by GMC Distribution Services,
Castle Place, 166 High Street, Lewes, East Sussex, England BN7 1XU

Distributed in Australia by Capricorn Link (Australia) Pty. Ltd.
P.O. Box 704, Windsor, NSW 2756, Australia

ISBN-13: 978-1-4027-3895-1
ISBN-10: 1-4027-3895-1

Printed in China

10 9 8 7 6 5 4 3 2 1

For information about custom editions, special sales, premium and
corporate purchases, please contact Sterling Special Sales
Department at 800-805-5489 or specialsales@sterlingpub.com.

Sterling Publishing Co., Inc.
New York

CELEBRATING

BOARD GAMES

By Nina Chertoff and Susan Kahn

Introduction

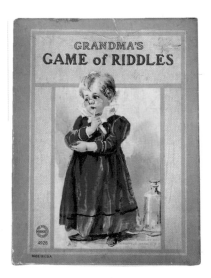

Grandma's Game of Riddles, late 1880s. Opposite, **Uncle Wiggily**, 1949.

Games are a part of almost everyone's childhood. And board games in particular have a special place in most people's hearts. They evoke treasured memories of hours playing Candyland or Checkers with family and friends. And as adults many of us still find pleasure in playing Scrabble and Clue and Monopoly. Many of today's newest games, of course, are electronic, and have to be attached to the back of a TV set or played on a computer. But once there was a time when detectives and knights glided across boards and conjured up visions of other worlds. So let's take a journey down a board game memory lane.

Every major ancient civilization has created board games, with the exception of the Australian Aborigines and the Eskimos. (It is, after all, hard to move pieces when it's 60 below.) The oldest known board game dates back to approximately 3500 B.C. and was found in a tomb in northern Egypt. There was no name on the game, needless to say, and we still don't know how it was played. One of the oldest games that we do know about which was

popular in ancient Egypt, was called Senat. It is credited with being the forerunner of our modern Backgammon. The Korean game of Nyout can be viewed as an ancient ancestor of Sorry, although Sorry had predecessors of similar design and mechanics in medieval Europe, and even in a game designed by American Indians.

Some of our newest games have links to the far-distant past. A good example is

Rudolph the Red-nosed Reindeer, 1948.

Atari. The company was named after a term used by masters of the ancient Chinese game Go. "Atari" is what the masters said after making a move that threatened their opponent. It is akin to "check" in Chess, a warning of impending capture.

In spite of these links to the past, the nature of games has changed considerably over the past 200 years. In many games prior to the mid-1800s, virtue was the reward in winning a board game. If you won, you were virtuous! After the mid-19th century and prior to the 1940s, being virtuous might help you win, but that was not in itself the reward—those rewards were now money, or promotion, or winning property or other material goods. Today, sadly, virtue plays little to no part in our gaming themes.

Games, then, are like snapshots of a society at a specific moment in time. Our interests, our imagination, and our values are all reflected in those simple boards and the pieces that move across them. Games have taken us through stock market booms and busts, and through cold wars and world wars. And they've taken us through what in retrospect seems the simpler times of the 1950s to the more complex times of today, when some of the more violent video games have even caught the attention of Congress.

In this wonderfully nostalgic book you will be treated to a great array of board games, ranging from Louisa in the 1800s, with its extraordinary box art, to the colorful art of 1950s board games like Merry Milkman and Fearless Fireman, to the action-filled games of today. And we've included a few card games as well. Just as illustrations of the period captured the essence of the times, so does the artwork in board games.

So turn the page and savor this enlightening and entertaining journey through the past.

Old Maid, 1950s.

Originally published in 1861, **Standard Authors** has been reissued many times and by many different companies. It is similar to Go Fish, but in this literary game the cards are authors. In a more educational version, players have to guess who the author is from information given to them about their works.

At right is the popular word game **Logomachy**, which first appeared in 1874. The original edition won the silver medal at the Cincinnati Industrial Exposition. The set shown here is from 1889, and a new version of the game has just been released.

A trio of early card games. Parker Brothers introduced the question-and-answer game **Komical Konversation Kards** in 1893. **Grandma's Game of Riddles** is one of several Grandma Games, all of which were educational. First published in the late 1880s, they must have given Grandmas hours of fun with their grandchildren. **The Game of Snap** was produced by several companies. Parker Brothers produced the one pictured here in 1905. At right is the **Game of Louisa**, introduced in 1888 by McLoughlin Bros. It was a variation of Parcheesi. Its artwork is particularly noteworthy.

Pollyanna
TRADE MARK

THE GLAD GAME

PARKER BROTHERS INC.

Another variant of Parcheesi, **Pollyanna** came out in 1915. Each edition featured a different woman with a different hairstyle from the period, all looking a bit like the early Breck shampoo models.

Eddie Cantor was a popular entertainer in the 1930s, but the game really had nothing to do with him, other than using his name and face on the box. Play involves cars, which were all the rage at the time. The exceptional graphics capture well this period in America.

14

EDDIE CANTOR'S GAME
"TELL IT TO THE JUDGE"

The goal of **Clipper Race** was to be the first to get around the globe (flattened as it was). Players used these terrific little ships for their markers. The game came out in the 1930s.

17

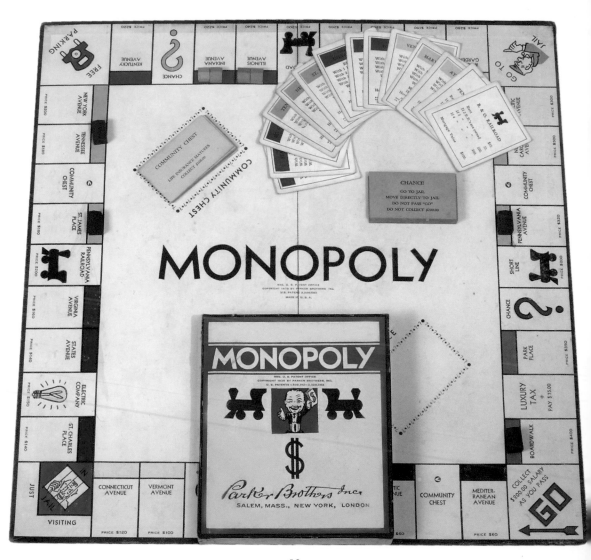

Appearing during the Great Depression, **Monopoly** allowed Americans to dream of financial success. The game's basic design is acknowledged to be similar to the "Landlord" game created by Elizabeth Maggie Phillips in 1904. But the Monopoly we know today, based on Atlantic City, is credited to Charles Darrow. Parker Brothers rejected his version of the game, so Mr. Darrow produced it himself and soon was selling thousands of sets. When production requirements overwhelmed his small company, he went back to Parker Brothers, and this time they listened—and bought. Over 200 million Monopoly games have been sold around the world, and it's believed that 500 million people have played it. These early metal tokens are treasured by collectors. (See also page 135.)

A great art-deco ship graces the box of **Cargoes**, which was produced in 1934 by Selchow & Richter. Players race around the world, stopping at various ports and collecting money. The first one back with the most money is the winner. **Finance** appeared in 1936 and was yet another game based on various ways to make money during this boom-and-bust period in American economic history.

While it did not rival Monopoly, **Bulls and Bears**, which mimics the workings of the stock market, did a great job of representing American capitalism in the late 1930s. **Pirate and Traveler** is a fantasy travel game that takes players to faraway places with a spin of the wheel. It was produced in the late 1930s. The graphics on the box and board are outstanding.

A backgammon game of In

PARCHEESI

TRADE MARK REG. U.S. PAT. OFF.

SEL RIGHT

POPULAR EDITION

PUBLISHERS
SELCHOW & RIGHTER CO.,
NEW YORK N Y MADE IN U.S.A.

People started playing **Parcheesi** in India in the 4th century. It is still a hugely popular game, based on luck and the throw of the dice. (See also page 140.)

At right is **The Lone Ranger**, a game inspired by the popular radio show of the 1930s. Years later came the well-loved TV show of the same name.

24

G U S H E R

If you were part of the women's movement in the 1960s, you might want to skip to the next page. In **Bizerte Gertie** there were four players, all servicemen on leave during World War II. Their goal was to take a walk with a beautiful woman on the beach; the object was not to be the player left with the "ugly" one (the token with the dog on it). Milton Bradley produced this, in a much different time.

The object of **Gusher** was pretty simple: making the most money from drilling for oil.

TALKS WITH FRIENDLY MONKEY · ADVANCE 2

MEETS 1ST TIGER LOSES RED COAT · · · BACK 1

ADMIRES SELF IN POOL · ADVANCE 1

START

A popular game in the 1940s and 1950s, **Little Black Sambo** is, in today's world, not only politically incorrect but offensive. The game was based on the book *Little Black Sambo* by Hellen Bannerman. It illustrates Sambo's adventures through the jungle as he tries not to be eaten by the animals. Each of the tigers would say, "Little Black Sambo, I'm going to eat you up." A period piece.

The object of **Touring** was to complete your automobile trip despite a variety of problems. Your opponents tried to slow you down with cards like "Puncture" or "Out of Gasoline." The game was first produced in 1906 and then by Parker Brothers in 1925. **Touring** is still available and is known today as Mille Borne.

The clever three-dimensional game of **Rudolph the Red-nosed Reindeer** was produced in 1948. Reindeers race to the top of the roof, according to the spin of the wheel, to see which will get to wear the big red nose.

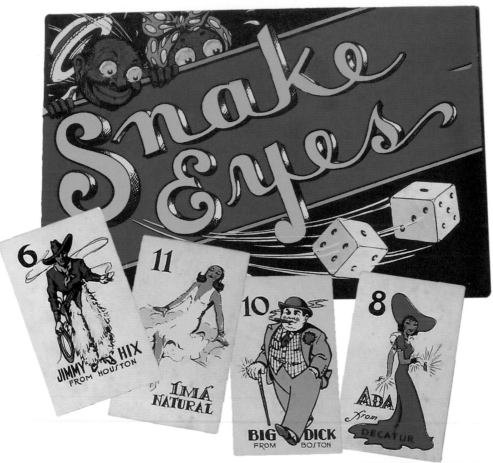

Snake Eyes is another period piece that has racial graphics that are unacceptable today. The game itself was a good one—a dice game with an escalating pot.

Calling All Cars was produced by Parker Brothers in 1949. The title is based on the popular movie phrase that summoned all police cars to the scene of a crime. Players move the metal cars around the board according to the spin of the wheel.

It's hard to find anyone who doesn't love **Clue**, the classic whodunit. Based on asking the right questions and using the process of elimination, this has been an American favorite since it was introduced in 1949. The artwork is almost film noir, and the weapon pieces are especially clever.

34

The object of **Cootie**, manufactured by Schaper, is to be the first player to complete making your cootie. You obtain pieces by rolling the dice, with each number representing a different body part. Cootie first appeared in 1949 and is still sold today.

A more educational game is **Lobby**, which teaches quite a bit about how Congress works. You might land on filibuster, or get your bill into the House or Senate.

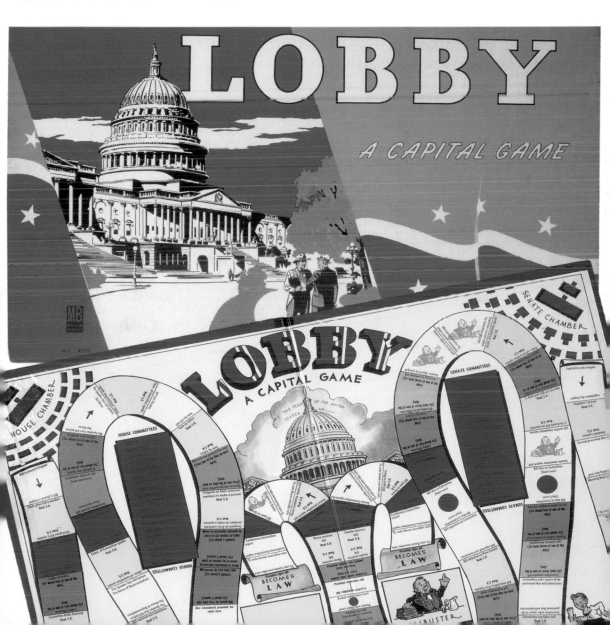

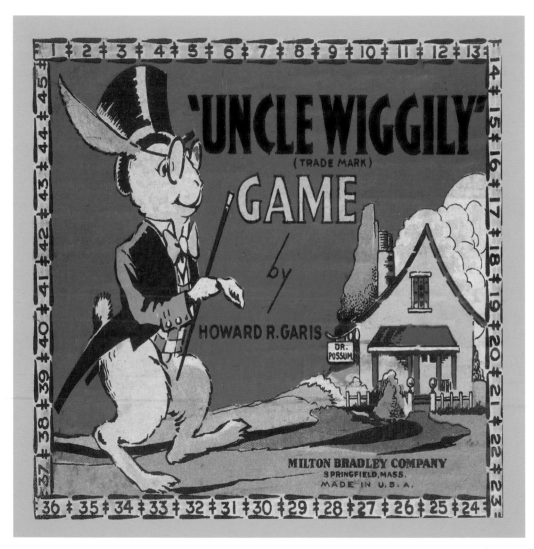

Based on a children's book first published in 1910, **Uncle Wiggily** was produced by Milton Bradley and has fabulous artwork. The beloved characters race to be the first to reach the end of the track.

Another well-loved, even iconic figure was **Hopalong Cassidy**, a cowboy made famous in the 1950s on TV. Players go around the board and collect reward money each time they find an outlaw. Escape routes make the game harder, and more fun. Go get 'em, Hoppy.

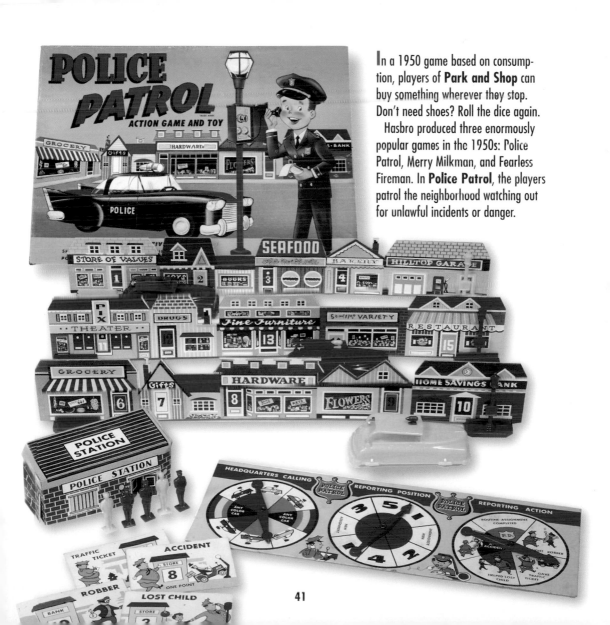

In a 1950 game based on consumption, players of **Park and Shop** can buy something wherever they stop. Don't need shoes? Roll the dice again.

Hasbro produced three enormously popular games in the 1950s: Police Patrol, Merry Milkman, and Fearless Fireman. In **Police Patrol**, the players patrol the neighborhood watching out for unlawful incidents or danger.

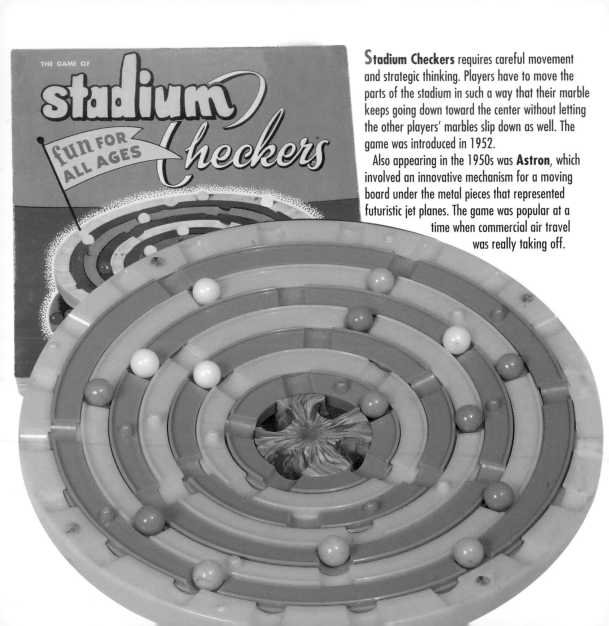

Stadium Checkers requires careful movement and strategic thinking. Players have to move the parts of the stadium in such a way that their marble keeps going down toward the center without letting the other players' marbles slip down as well. The game was introduced in 1952.

Also appearing in the 1950s was **Astron**, which involved an innovative mechanism for a moving board under the metal pieces that represented futuristic jet planes. The game was popular at a time when commercial air travel was really taking off.

THE GAME OF

stadium

Checkers

fun FOR ALL AGES

43

In a game similar to Cootie, the object of **Dunce** was to be the first (or perhaps the last!) to put your Dunce together. You obtained pieces by spinning the top. The game was produced by Schaper and came out in 1955.

Davy Crockett came to fame as part of the 1950s TV show *Disneyland*. Five episodes featured Fess Parker as Davy Crockett, and are considered TV's first miniseries. The wildly successful show inspired this tie-in game, **Frontierland.**

RAL STORE
Walt Disney's
OFFICIAL
Frontierland
GAME
Parker Brothers Inc
Walt Disney's
Frontierland
GAME

Merry Milkman appeared in 1955, seemingly a kinder, gentler time. Players move around the board doling out eggs, milk, and cheese. The graphics and pieces are reminiscent of an idyllic age in American history.

Prince Valiant was a well-known comic strip, then a movie, and in 1954 became a game. The object was to reach the castle first and be named a knight.

Gabby
Gob

Old
Maid

45 CARDS
OF PLAYING CARD QUALITY

OLD MAID

No. 3009 ★ MADE IN U.S.A., WHITMAN

Dora
Dubb

48

Sassiety
Sal

Broncho Buster

Flighty Fanny

Steppin' Sam

Tooty Tutor

Gurgling Gertie

Stella Steno

Old Maid is thought to have first appeared in the late 1890s. The object is not to get stuck with the Old Maid card after all the pairs in the deck have been matched. There are many editions of the game. The one pictured here, with its delightful graphics, is from the mid-1950s.

Most youngsters in the 1950s were familiar with a TV show about a heroic German shepherd. The tie-in **Rin-Tin-Tin** game let them get their own bad guys and become the hero. It was first produced in 1955 by Transogram.

In 1956, when **Tomorrowland** appeared, there was great optimism about our ability to someday reach the moon. Disney produced **Fantasyland** at about the same time it opened its first theme park in California in 1955. Children who couldn't get to the park could visit it through these fun board games.

Ellery Queen is the hero of **Trapped!**, a 1950s mystery game with a 3-D molded board. Six could play, and there were also six bodies, six fingerprints, six motive chips, and six clocks. The cover has terrific graphics.

Released in 1957, **Around the World in 80 Days** was based on the popular movie of the same name. This was another game that celebrated America's new obsession with foreign travel.

A popular spin game, **Fearless Fireman** let players get to be firemen and save people from burning buildings. The game is wonderfully emblematic of the 1950s.

Children could watch their elegant horses speed through the racetrack as they spun the fabulous wheel on **Thrills 'n' Spills**.

Walt Disney's stunning graphics in **Sleeping Beauty** perfectly capture the magic of the fairy tale. In this traditional board game you spin your way toward the castle and the kiss. Way before Woodward and Bernstein, America was tantalized by reporters and getting a scoop. **Star Reporter** appeared in 1958; it let children race from city to city and compete for the front-page story.

Many games capitalized on the success of a movie or TV show. **Why** used parodies of some favorite sleuths in this murder mystery game. Produced in 1958, it was all directed by Alfred Hitchcock, featured on the cover.

He must be the least scary ghost ever, and when **Casper** came out in 1959 he was certainly the most popular. The winner was the first to enter the haunted house.

A different game entirely, though from the same year, was **Have Gun Will Travel**, which was based on a popular TV western. Paladin, a hired gun, was the hero. You won points if you captured the outlaw and even more points if you killed him.

65

Cherry Ames' Nursing Game, from the 1950s, was based on the very popular Cherry Ames books. The goal was to move around the board in ways that would ensure you successfully finished nursing school. Complete with instructions from a (presumably male) doctor to wipe off the rouge, this is another game that would not be considered politically correct today.

Cherry Ames' NURSING *Game*

Parker Brothers Inc.
SALEM, MASSACHUSETTS
NEW YORK • CHICAGO • SAN — • ATLANTA

A box of lollipops gets Cherry into trouble. **Move back 5 spaces.**

Cherry watches her first operation. Take any ring from the board.

Cherry gives up the Nurses' Dance to relieve on night duty. — spaces ahead.

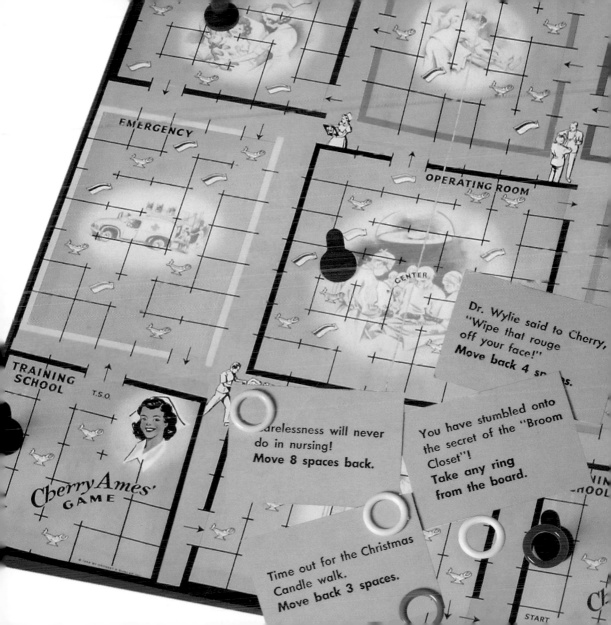

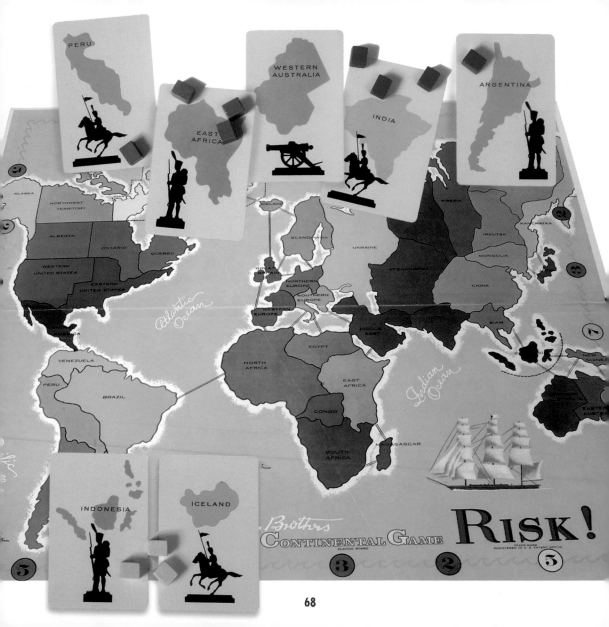

In 1959, Parker Brothers created **Risk!**, considered to be the first popular world conquest game—still available in various versions.

Another military game starred **Steve Canyon**, a popular comic book character. The tokens are models of the F-105. The game is based on pilot Steve getting safely to his destination despite obstacles like storms and low fuel.

70

Sure to bring a nostalgic smile to many faces, **Go to the Head of the Class** is a beloved board game that is still going strong. The game lets children show off their school smarts to friends and parents. The one pictured here is from the 1950s.

A classic Milton Bradley game that was introduced in 1960, **The Game of Life** let you spin the wheel to make critical decisions that would determine where you would end up at the end of the game (of life).

Camelot is a version of a chess game that stars Sir Lancelot's knights. The original version was produced in 1930. The one pictured here is from 1961.

The artwork in **Tally Ho!**, a 1961 game, is fun. The hound is racing after the fox—spin and catch him.

In **Lucky Loopy**, players had an opportunity to turn their house into a mini-carnival. Children would throw the ball at the donkey to turn the panels over. Presumably, someone got the vases out of the way.

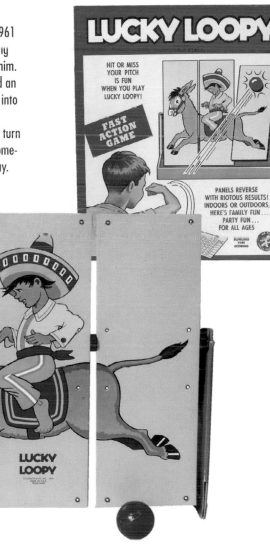

Combat! appeared in 1963. Based on a TV show about World War II that was also called *Combat!*, the game featured pieces that were standing soldiers, weapons in hand, ready to pounce.

  Shown at right is the 1964 edition of **Sorry!**, the classic Parker Brothers game originally published in England. It didn't arrive on our shores until 1934. Sorry!, a variant of Parcheesi, has been hugely popular since it first came out.

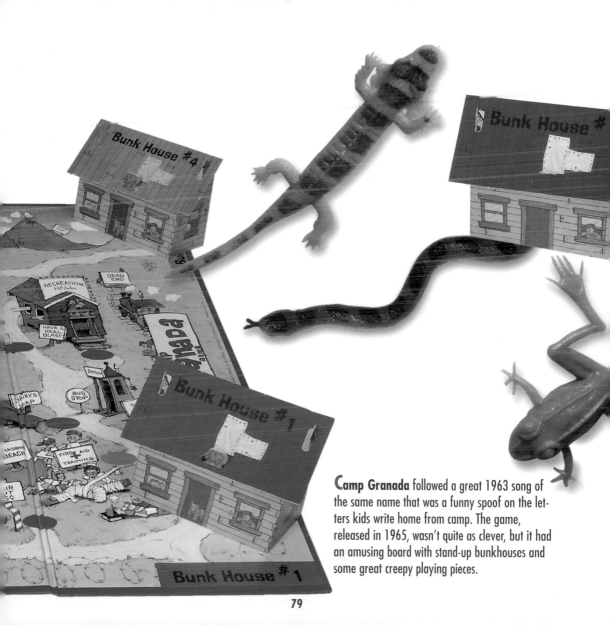

Camp Granada followed a great 1963 song of the same name that was a funny spoof on the letters kids write home from camp. The game, released in 1965, wasn't quite as clever, but it had an amusing board with stand-up bunkhouses and some great creepy playing pieces.

First came the sleek and coy TV show. In 1965 the board game **The Man from U.N.C.L.E.** was developed and was pretty sleek as well—a class act, just like Robert Vaughn in the starring role of Napoleon Solo.

And speaking of Napoleon, at right is a 1966 chess set starring the emperor himself.

The knights are at it again in **Siege**. Storm the castle, capture anyone you can.

In **Fu Manchu's Hidden Hoard**, Western men in business suits looked for hidden treasures in spooky locations. In their pursuit they had to confront a nefarious-looking Chinese man; but remember, China was a land of great mystery to Americans in the 1960s.

Though the pieces in **Regatta** seem to resemble fried eggs more than islands, youngsters and adults alike could get into this extremely exciting yacht-racing game from 1968. Watch out for those sudden wind changes!

Don't play **Kreskin's ESP** with anyone but a really good friend, because Kreskin will show you how to see into the other player's mind. This elaborate and fun game was very popular in 1967.

A favorite of many, **Dominoes** is one of the oldest games in the world. This is a 1970 version.

DOUBLE SIX DOMINOES
DOMINOES
• 28 QUALITY ENGRAVED DOMINOES
• CONVENIENT STORAGE BOX
• INSTRUCTIONS INCLUDED

The paintings in **Masterpiece: The Art Auction Game** were worth a fortune when this game came out in 1970. Today they would be worth at least 10 times more and the makers would have to add more money chips. The game is a fun way to simulate participating in an art auction.

MASTERPIECE
The Art Auction Game
by Parker Brothers

to 6 players

V. Elton Whitehall

Once London's top criminal lawyer. De
indicted in 3 million pound train robbe
freed. The Barrister retired to his S
Immediately thereafter. Cautious, cons
smilingly feared in highly cultured
rently maintains fabulous estates in
Majorca and Northern-most Finland.
orange Bentley.

© 1970 Parker Brothers, Inc., Salem, Mass. 01970

COUNT FRANCOIS DU BONNET

One of the most popular figures on the continent.
Crafty, cunning, charming beyond belief. During
the Nazi occupation, the Count worked with
French groups posing as an enemy collaborator
when the Louvre was sacked. Still some question
as to whether the Germans stole genuines or
forgeries. Made headlines in 1951 when he pur-
chased an unknown original Rembrandt for 34
francs.

© 1970 Parker Brothers, Inc., Salem, Mass. 01970   M806 in U.S.A

Millicent Friendly

Spinster librarian from Central City. Wo
trip to Omaha in 1947 where she was first
to great art. Later inherited modest sum
secret admirer and parlayed it into severa
through cautious, skilled investment in art
ingly shy and unassuming, but reputed to
mean temper.

89

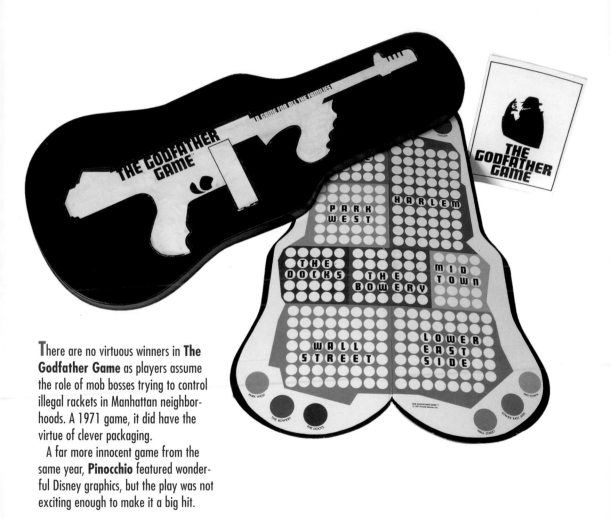

There are no virtuous winners in **The Godfather Game** as players assume the role of mob bosses trying to control illegal rackets in Manhattan neighborhoods. A 1971 game, it did have the virtue of clever packaging.

A far more innocent game from the same year, **Pinocchio** featured wonderful Disney graphics, but the play was not exciting enough to make it a big hit.

Do you believe in the supernatural? If so, **Ouija** is your game. Place your hand on the three-legged pointer and it moves seemingly by itself to various letters as it mysteriously answers your questions. The first Ouija board was invented in 1890. The one here is from 1972.

Hare and Tortoise was produced in 1973. The game has wonderful graphics and requires some mathematical calculations and cunning to win.

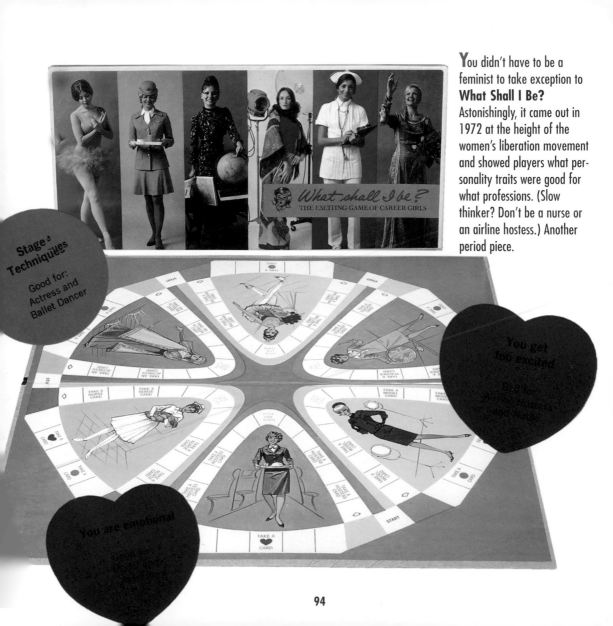

You didn't have to be a feminist to take exception to **What Shall I Be?** Astonishingly, it came out in 1972 at the height of the women's liberation movement and showed players what personality traits were good for what professions. (Slow thinker? Don't be a nurse or an airline hostess.) Another period piece.

What shall I be?
THE EXCITING GAME OF CAREER GIRLS

Stage Techniques
Good for:
Actress and Ballet Dancer

You get too excited
Bad for Airline Hostess and Nurse

You are emotional
Good for: Model and Actress

COLLEGE

Teacher

AIRLINE TRAINING SCHOOL

DRAMA SCHOOL

Actress

Correct Posture

Good for:
Airline Hostess,
Ballet Dancer,
Actress and
Model

**You are
not considerate**

Bad for:
Airline Hostess,
Nurse and
Teacher

NURSING SCHOOL

Nurse

BALLET SCHOOL

Ballet Dancer

CHARM SCHOOL

Model

**You failed
English**

Bad for:
Teacher and
Actress

**You are
a slow thinker**

Bad for:
Airline Hostess
and Nurse

Checkers and **Chinese Checkers** are here combined in one clever, attractive package.

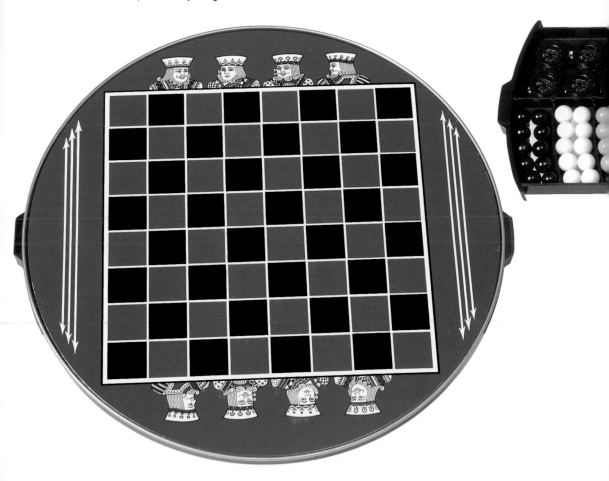

Creature Features is really Monopoly-like with a horror-movie theme. Players move around the board buying up movies and movie houses and receive cards featuring favorite characters.

The game of **Cracker Jack** did not live up to the incredible popularity of its namesake. Players would spin a large Cracker Jack box, hoping to match cards with prizes hidden under smaller Cracker Jack boxes. The player with the best memory would obtain the most surprises and win the game.

CARRIER STRIKE!

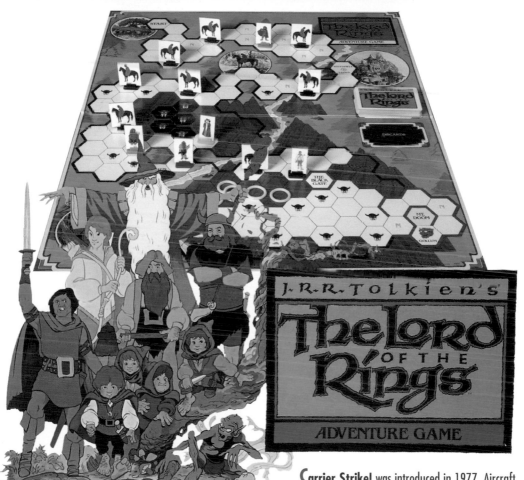

Carrier Strike! was introduced in 1977. Aircraft carrier task forces compete against each other, maneuvering to avoid deadly torpedo-plane attacks.

Pick your hobbit and begin to play **The Lord of the Rings**. The game came out in 1978 when the first animated movie in the series was released.

John Hill, a respected war-game designer, conceived of **Panzerforce**, which is based on tank-to-tank combat during World War II.

On the other end of the spectrum is **Winnie the Pooh**, a simple game based on selecting colorful plastic discs from a bag and moving them around the board. This version of the game has the same sweet design as the original, which appeared in 1933.

Great graphics and the zany twists of rolling the dice with your left hand and moving counterclockwise made **The Mad Magazine Game** fun. It was similar to Monopoly, but with a whole different look.

Candyland, first produced in 1949, has long been considered "the" first game for children. It teaches little ones to take turns and introduces them to simple rules for moving around a board. Children—and their parents—love the graphics and the simplicity.

Dark Tower is a popular electronic game from Milton Bradley. It was first introduced in 1981 and is still in demand today at online auction sites. Find the three keys to the tower, enter, and vanquish the evil therein! The tower contains a small computer that controls the game play.

Two ships face off against each other in **Broadsides & Boarding Parties**, a game of high adventure. It's the first in Milton Bradley's Gamemaster series and has relatively simple rules. The board is beautifully designed, and the well crafted pieces include a big ship and several crew members.

A noncaloric way to indulge in that old favorite, **Barnum's Animal Crackers**. The simple spin game comes with cute animal pieces.

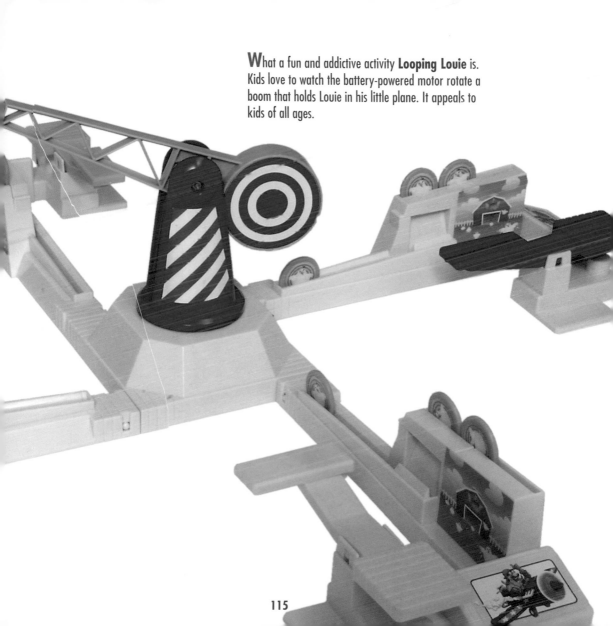

What a fun and addictive activity **Looping Louie** is. Kids love to watch the battery-powered motor rotate a boom that holds Louie in his little plane. It appeals to kids of all ages.

Wadjet is an archaeologist's version of Clue. Players have to discover what is in the tombs without disturbing the spirits. It is a lot of fun, with great character pieces. It appeared in 1994, just before electronic games with similar themes exploded in popularity.

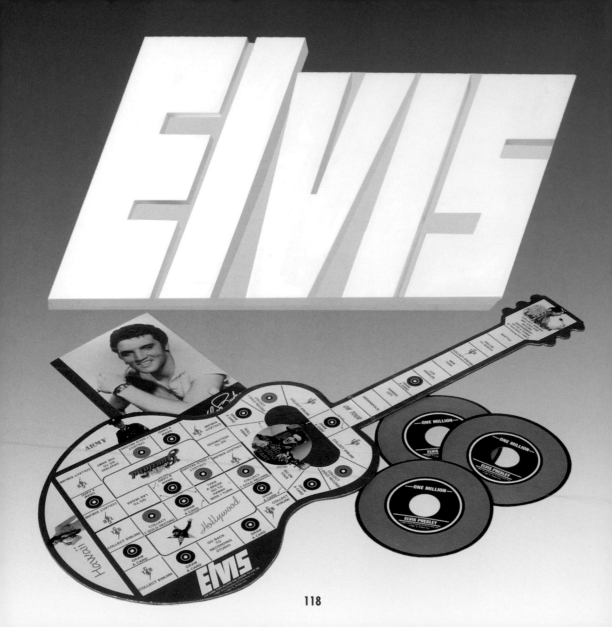

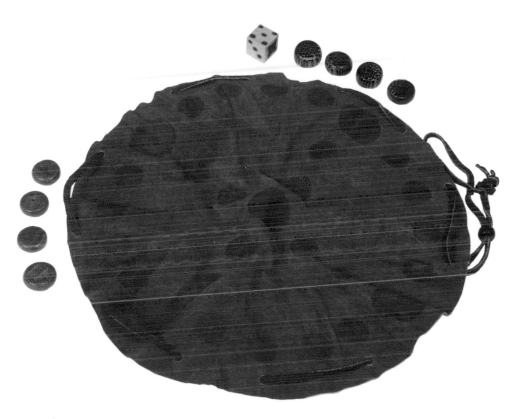

If you love all things **Elvis**, this is the game for you. The box is a white plastic mold of the King's name, the board is shaped like a guitar, and the playing pieces include a pink Cadillac, a pair of blue suede shoes, and a hound dog. The cards look like 45-rpm records, and the rules are printed on a cutout of Graceland. It is highly collectible.

   Nyout (above) is a forefather of Sorry. The game pictured here is a reproduction of a medieval version that first appeared in Korea in the 3rd century.

Despite its early-20th-century look, **Aeronautika** was produced in the mid-1990s in Europe. Visually stunning, with well-crafted plane models, it vividly recreates the time of those first flights over the English Channel.

Surprisingly enough, **Mississippi Queen** was produced in Europe. Players race down the twists and turns of the swirling Mississippi River.

Dinosaurier was manufactured in Germany in 1996. Players' armies of men and dinosaurs battle it out through the play of various action cards.

Clue as only the Simpson gang could play it. The suspects are Homer, Marge, Bart, Lisa, Krusty the Clown, and Waylon Smithers.

Pictured at right is a nice nostalgia edition set.

A beautifully executed German racing game, **TurfMaster** was produced in 1998. The horse-and-jockey pieces are of very high quality.

5 6 7 8

As addictive today as it was when Parker Brothers introduced it in 1979, **Can't Stop** is a classic dice game by Sid Jackson, considered one of America's greatest game designers. Players compete to complete three columns and have to decide whether to stop and secure their progress or keep rolling the dice.

Hasbro produced **Battle Cry**, an elegant Civil War game, in 2000. Well-known Civil War battles are fought with Union and Confederate troops.

Produced in 2000 by the same European company as TurfMaster, AZA Spiele, **MotorChamp** is considered by experts to be one of the best games on the market. It comes with various boards that allow players to create twelve different tracks.

Hamster Rolle is a game of dexterity that came from Europe in 2000. Players add pieces to the wheel that cause it to turn slowly. The object of the game is to get rid of all of your pieces. But be careful—pieces will fall off.

There are hundreds of packaging options for the game of **Monopoly**. Shown at right are two nice wooden-box editions and another in a 3-D metal container.

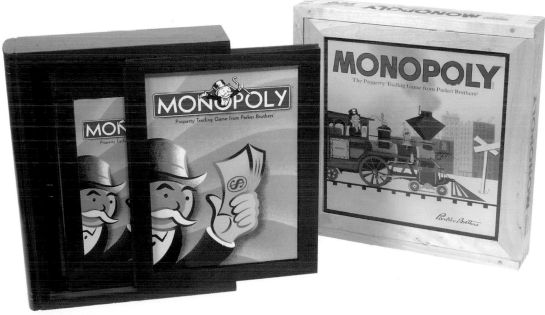

If you missed it on the news, you can see it here. Players get caught in violence in the walkways of a neighborhood mall in **Mall of Horror**. This game has graphics and goals that are very similar to today's electronic games.

SECURITY CAMERAS

HARDWARE

GRENADES

HIDDEN

Niagara is set in 18th-century America. Adventurers compete with each other for a cache of jewels, all the while contending with a raging river, changing weather, and other obstacles. This very American game was manufactured in Germany in 2000.

Gangsters split their loot in **Cash 'n Guns**. Money—and guns—talk, and soon everyone is shooting at everyone else. The richest surviving bad guy wins.

Another version of **Parcheesi**, this one (left) has graphics that recall India, the land where the popular game began many centuries ago.

Villa Paletti is a fun game that appeared in 2001. Future architects and builders use their balancing skills to create a fanciful, colorful tower. A steady hand is needed to prevent the tower from collapsing.

Celebrating Our Collector

We are grateful to **Tony Elam** for allowing us
to photograph a small part of his vast collection
of games, and for graciously providing us with
so much fascinating information about their history. All of the games featured in this
book are from his incredible collection, which currently num-
bers more than 6,200.

Tony is the Associate
Dean of Engineering
at Rice University in
Houston, Texas. He
is an avid game collec-
tor and player, and is
interested in both the history of games and the use
of games in education. He is
currently the Director of Games in
Education for the Game Manufacturers
Association.

Game List

BINGO

Barbara J. Morgan Publisher
Leonard Vigliarolo Design Director
Robert Milazzo Photography
Jane F. Neighbors Copy Editor
Gina Graham Editorial Assistant
James Trimarco Art Assistant
Della R. Mancuso Production